A SEASON FOR CHANGE

Praying the Gospels of Lent

Philip St. Romain

LIGUORI
PUBLICATIONS

One Liguori Drive
Liguori, MO 63057-9999
(314) 464-2500

Imprimi Potest:
James Shea, C.SS.R.
Provincial, St. Louis Province
The Redemptorists

Imprimatur:
+ Edward J. O'Donnell, D.D.
Auxiliary Bishop, Archdiocese of St. Louis

ISBN 0-89243-789-8
Library of Congress Catalog Card Number: 94-79994

Scripture quotations are taken from the *New American Bible*, Copyright
© 1970, 1986, and 1991 by the Confraternity of Christian Doctrine, 3211
Fourth Street, N.E., Washington, DC 20017-1194, and are used with per-
mission. All rights reserved.

Portions of this booklet were excerpted from *Praying the Daily Gospels: A
Guide to Meditation* by Philip St. Romain, formerly published by Ave Maria
Press, Notre Dame, Indiana.

Cover design by Myra Roth

CONTENTS

INTRODUCTION

Lent was originally the season when catechumens—those preparing to come into the Church—devoted themselves to more time for prayer and reflection. It was an extended retreat of sorts, in which the heart was purged of all unnecessary attachments so as to make room to receive Christ in baptism and the Eucharist at the Easter Vigil. Through the centuries, the larger community came to recognize the value of devoting a period of time to this kind of discipline. Lent became, for the whole Church, a season for growing closer to God through prayer, fasting, and almsgiving.

Using the psalms and gospel readings from the Church's liturgy as the basis for meditation, this booklet is intended as a resource for the Christian who wants to grow in prayer during Lent. Unlike many other Lenten prayer guides, this one does not provide a meditation for you. Instead, it offers suggestions for your own reflection. Each daily entry features a psalm, a short commentary on the gospel of the day, as well as questions and suggestions to enhance your meditation.

As Saint Alphonsus so beautifully put it, "Prayer is talking to God about the things that pertain to our friendship." I hope this booklet will help deepen your friendship with God, bringing new richness to this most important relationship of all.

HOW TO PRAY WITH SCRIPTURE

To make the most of this opportunity to grow in your relationship with God, I recommend that you set aside at least twenty minutes every day for prayer. For most people, first thing in the morning works best. That way, the fruit of their prayer nourishes them all day. If early morning is not possible, find another time that will work for you. And, of course, if you want to go beyond twenty minutes, that would be wonderful!

Having chosen your time, you should be faithful to the disciplines of solitude and silence. While there is a time and a place for communal prayer, this time is to be spent alone with God, to develop your own friendship with him so you will be able to share this with others in communal prayer. Try to find a place where it will be quiet. Get away from the phone, and turn off the television and radio. Tell your family that unless it is an emergency, you do not want to be disturbed.

For your time of silence and solitude with God, I recommend the following method of praying with Scripture:

1. **Quieting.** Take a few moments to settle in. Find a comfortable position, and ask the Holy Spirit to lead you in this time of prayer. Let your mind become calm by noticing your bodily sensations, the sounds in the room around you, the rhythm and feel of your own breathing. Do not be disturbed if your mind does not become completely silent. It hardly ever will.

2. **Listening.** When you are ready, pick up the Bible and read the psalm for the day. This will help to direct your thoughts toward God. Pause briefly, and then read the short commentary on the gospel of the day. Now read the gospel slowly and prayerfully, as though it were a letter from God to you. If a particular word or phrase from the passage speaks to you, pause with it for a while, repeating this word or phrase in your mind or on your lips. Let its meaning penetrate you deeply.

3. **Prayer.** When you are ready, tell God in your own words what this word or passage means to you. It can be in the form of a feeling, a question, a petition, or maybe just loving silence. Continue reading the passage, pausing at meaningful words and phrases and responding in prayer until you have finished the reading, or until you are out of time.

4. **Reflection.** If time permits, or if you find few words or phrases that hold your attention for very long, consider the questions and suggestions for meditation. You might find it beneficial to record your responses in a journal or notebook.

5. **Resolution.** As a result of this time of listening, praying, and reflecting, what will you strive to do (or not to do) today? A suggested resolution—in the form of a prayer for a particular grace—is provided for most days.

6. **Loving Silence.** Conclude your prayer time by resting in the awareness of God's love for you. You do not need to say anything during this time. Just open your heart and your mind to God, and allow the fruit of your prayer to take root in your being. If you enjoy this experience of resting in God, extend your prayer time to allow it to deepen.

WEEK OF ASH WEDNESDAY

Ash Wednesday

Psalm 51:3-6,12-14,17
Matthew 6:1-6,16-18: *Be sincere!*

Gaining the esteem of others is something we all desire, but Jesus makes it clear that our religious acts should be done to bring us closer to God, not to impress people. Some of the examples of hypocrisy he gives refer to practices of the Pharisees.

- How important is it to you that others know you are committed to following Jesus Christ? What are your motives for letting others know that you are a Christian?

- In what ways does your heavenly Father repay you for your personal prayer? Spend some time thanking God for these graces.

Thursday After Ash Wednesday

Psalm 1:1-6
Luke 9:22-25: *Take up your cross!*

Jesus tried to help his disciples realize that his commitment to love would lead him into a fatal conflict with the authorities of his day. Dying to ourselves for the sake of love will lead us, with Jesus, to new life.

- Make a list of those personal traits which you need to change for the sake of love. Which of these most frustrates your efforts at loving?

- Pray for the grace to change destructive behaviors.

Friday After Ash Wednesday

Psalm 51:3-6,18-19
Matthew 9:14-15: *Jesus the bridegroom*

Jesus viewed his coming as a time of grace, and he believed that this ought to be celebrated. Many times he likened God's kingdom to a wedding feast, where people rejoiced and had fun. The day would come, however, when fasting would be appropriate. That time is now.

- Read Isaiah 58:1-9—today's first reading—for a better understanding of the kind of fast that God desires. How can you better exemplify this spirit of fasting in your lifestyle?

- Pray for the grace to hunger for the things of God.

Saturday After Ash Wednesday

Psalm 86:1-6
Luke 5:27-32: *The call of Levi*

Tax collectors were men commissioned by the Romans to exact from the peoples they governed monies and property owed Rome. Then, as now, tax collectors were despised by the people. Levi, a Jew, was considered a traitor by other Jews, but Jesus nonetheless chose him to be a disciple, a member of his inner circle. Jesus' call elicited gratitude from Levi and scandalized the Pharisees and scribes.

- What does Jesus mean when he talks of "healthy" and "sick" people? In which group do you consider yourself, and why?

- Spend some time re-creating this scene in your imagination. Sense the rejection Levi feels from his fellow Jews; note the change when he sees Jesus paying attention to him; hear Jesus saying to him—and to you—"Follow me."

FIRST WEEK OF LENT

First Sunday of Lent

CYCLE A

Psalm 51:3-6,12-14,17
Matthew 4:1-11: *Temptation in the wilderness*

Like every human being, Jesus, too, was tempted. In today's gospel, Satan tries to steer Jesus off course by inviting him to use his divine authority to attain personal pleasure, temporal power, and security. Jesus resists all three temptations and affirms the primacy of the love of God.

- What temptation(s) most frequently lead you away from a life centered on God?

- What do you need to do to strengthen your resistance to temptation?

- Pray for the grace to resist some specific temptation today.

CYCLE B

Psalm 25:4-9
Mark 1:12-15: *Jesus begins his ministry*

Mark does not give us much detail about Jesus' temptation in the wilderness. Nor does the message of Jesus seem very different from that already preached by John the Baptist. But the themes of God's providence and the coming of the kingdom will feature prominently in the story Mark is telling.

- How do you experience God's providence in your life? Do you believe you will always have what you need when you need it? Why or why not?

- Spend some time with the passage, "This is the time of fulfillment. The kingdom of God is at hand. Repent, and believe in the gospel" (Mark 1:15). From what do you need to repent? How do you experience the kingdom as close at hand?

CYCLE C

Psalm 91:1-2,10-15
Luke 4:1-13: *Jesus is tempted*

Before beginning his public ministry, Jesus "makes a retreat." In the wilderness, he encounters Satan, who goes so far as to quote Scripture in order to thwart his mission. Jesus sees through these ruses, however, and leaves the desert filled with the Holy Spirit.

- How does Jesus counter the temptations that are couched in the language of Scripture? Why is it important to know both the content and meaning of Scripture?

- What kind of temptation(s) have you been experiencing lately? What do you need to do to strengthen yourself to resist them?

- Pray for the grace to resist temptation.

Monday of the First Week of Lent

Psalm 19:8-10,15
Matthew 25:31-46: *Who are the saved?*

It has often been said that the clearest indication of our relationship with God may be deduced from our relationships with other people. In today's reading, Jesus makes it clear that we will be judged on the basis of how we have treated others—especially society's outcasts.

- If you were to die today, do you believe you would be included in the company of the sheep, or that of the goats?

- Is there any person or any ethnic or religious group against whom you harbor resentments and make harsh judgments?

- Pray for the grace to see all people as children of God.

Tuesday of the First Week of Lent

Psalm 34:4-7,16-19
Matthew 6:7-15: *The Lord's Prayer*

This most famous of all prayers is rather a formula for prayer. Its movements include acknowledgment and praise of God as creator, hope for the kingdom, affirmation of the importance of life on earth, petition for our needs, and requests for forgiveness of sin and protection from evil. This passage concludes with a sobering reminder that our experience of God's forgiveness is contingent on our own willingness to forgive.

- Spend a few moments with each line of the Lord's Prayer, adding your own prayers to each verse. When you ask for your daily bread and for forgiveness of your sins, be specific in your requests.

Wednesday of the First Week of Lent

Psalm 51:3-4,12-13,18-19
Luke 11:29-32: *The sign of Jonah*

Jesus' condemnation of the attitude of the crowds was intended to move them to faith. He saw that they did not really hunger for the things of God, but wanted demonstrations of supernatural power instead. The Queen of Sheba and the Ninevites were pagans who recognized the workings of God in his people and who reformed their lives accordingly. Jesus holds them out as models for us.

- What are some signs of God's presence that are most meaningful to you? What signs must you try harder to recognize?

- Pray for the grace to recognize God at work in yourself and others.

Thursday of the First Week of Lent

Psalm 138:1-3,7-8
Matthew 7:7-12: *Ask, seek, knock*

Jesus reveals to us a God who is generous and responsive. This does not exempt us, however, from searching for ways to grow closer to God. It is in the searching and asking that we discover ourselves, as well as God's goodness.

- What are you seeking from God? from your family members?

- How would you like others to treat you? Make a list, and then resolve to treat others likewise.

Friday of the First Week of Lent

Psalm 130:1-8
Matthew 5:20-26: *On forgiveness and reconciliation*

Today's reading introduces an important lesson. We learn that anger can separate us from others, and therefore we ought to control it by striving to be reconciled with those who are the objects of our anger.

- Who or what most often causes you anger? How do you usually handle your anger? Are your expectations of others always reasonable? How might you alter your expectations?

- Make a commitment to reconcile with someone with whom you are angry (or who is angry with you).

Saturday of the First Week of Lent

Psalm 119:1-8
Matthew 5:43-48: *Love your enemies*

Jesus teaches that the only way to break the seemingly endless cycle of hatred and revenge is to begin to treat enemies as fellow children of God. The commandment to love our enemies is one of the most unique of all Jesus' teachings and, unfortunately, the most neglected as well.

- The eighteenth-century French satirist Voltaire wrote that patriotism really means hating every other country but your own. Do you sense this kind of spirit in the world around you? How does it affect you?

- Spend some time in prayer for people with whom you do not get along particularly well. Ask for the grace to begin to love them.

SECOND WEEK OF LENT

Second Sunday of Lent

CYCLE A

Psalm 33:4-5,18-22
Matthew 17:1-9: *Jesus is transfigured*

Peter, James, and John were the three apostles with whom Jesus chose to share most deeply. In order to strengthen their faith and prepare them for the resurrection, they were given on Mount Tabor a glimpse of Jesus in his glory. The presence of Moses and Elijah affirm that Jesus is the Messiah.

- Spend a few moments recalling a very happy event in your life. How was God present to you in this experience?

- Pray for the grace to be open to the joy in life.

CYCLE B

Psalm 116:10,15-19
Mark 9:2-10: *Jesus' glory is revealed*

Many commentators assert that the glorious vision Peter, James, and John witnessed had little to do with a change brought about in Jesus. Rather, the change was in the perception of the apostles themselves. For a brief moment, they were given to see Jesus as he always was.

- How do preconceptions keep you from seeing people and circumstances as they really are?

- Pray for the grace to be more open to and accepting of the good in others and the beauty of life.

CYCLE C

Psalm 27:1, 7-9, 13-14
Luke 9:28-36: *The Transfiguration*

This glorious manifestation of Jesus is similar to the theophanies that Moses witnessed on Mount Sinai. Peter, James, and John are the leaders of the New Covenant. Instead of giving them commandments written on stone tablets, God tells them to listen to Jesus.

- How do you listen to Jesus in your daily life? What can you do to listen to him more closely?

- Invite Jesus to speak to you in your thoughts. Begin by asking him a question or making a petition, and then let your meditation proceed as if he were the one speaking.

- Pray for the desire to be a good disciple.

Monday of the Second Week of Lent

Psalm 79:8-9,11,13
Luke 6:36-38: *Do not judge*

Today's reading is one of the most sobering in Scripture. Jesus proposes that we evaluate our lives using the same criteria we use to evaluate others. How do we fare?

- Old sayings have it that "What goes around comes around" and "You will get out of life no more nor less than you put into it." Are these true in your experience?

- Why are Christians called to be compassionate?

- Pray for the grace to see others as God sees them.

Tuesday of the Second Week of Lent

Psalm 50:8-9,16-17,21,23
Matthew 23:1-12: *On servant leadership*

The principle of servant leadership has it that one's ability to use authority responsibly stands in direct relationship with one's service to others. Authority assumed for reasons other than service will result in all kinds of abuses and superficialities.

- Which title best fits Jesus: king, ruler, servant, master, prophet, teacher, philosopher, rabbi? Why did you choose the one you did?

- Do you think of yourself as a servant? Whom do you serve?

Wednesday of the Second Week of Lent

Psalm 31:5-6,14-16
Matthew 20:17-28: *A mother's request*

It is obvious to us today that the mother of Zebedee's sons did not understand what Jesus' kingdom was about. Her request was made in good faith—not an unusual one from a Jewish mother trying to see to it that her sons get the best treatment possible. Jesus turns the indignation that followed into a teachable moment.

- What are some of your professional ambitions? How important is it that you achieve them? Why?

- Pray for the grace to accept failure, as well as success.

Thursday of the Second Week of Lent

Psalm 1:1-4,6
Luke 16:19-31: *The rich man and Lazarus*

The parable of the Rich Man and Lazarus teaches us that the real value of our lives must be weighed against the inevitability of death and the prospect of judgment before God. The surest way to guarantee repose in the "bosom of Abraham" is to love God and neighbor.

- What kinds of situations make you feel insecure? When do you feel most secure? What is the primary source of your security?

- How do you feel about the prospect of coming before God's judgment when you die?

Friday of the Second Week of Lent

Psalm 105:16-21
Matthew 21:33-46: *Parable of the wicked tenants*

Jesus did not hide behind polite facades when love required that the truth be spoken. In today's parable, he reveals his knowledge of the intentions of certain Jewish authorities to dispose of him, yet continues to invite them to recognize God working through him.

- God has entrusted us with the cultivation of a vineyard, his kingdom. Who are the faithful tenants today? Who are the unfaithful? How can you tell one from the other?

- If the Master of the vineyard were to come today, what do you think he would say to you? Spend some time listening.

Saturday of the Second Week of Lent

Psalm 103:1-4,9-12
Luke 15:1-3,11-32: *The Prodigal Son*

Today's parable is extremely rich in meaning. The marked contrasts between the attitudes of the father, the faithful son, and the prodigal son tell us much about God and ourselves.

- List some of the areas in your life where you are faithful to God. List as well a few of the reasons *why* you are faithful in each of these areas.

- Write a short characterization of the father in the parable.

- Pray for the grace to know that you are a forgiven sinner.

THIRD WEEK OF LENT

Third Sunday of Lent

CYCLE A

Psalm 95:1-2,6-9
John 4:5-42: *Conversion of a Samaritan woman*

No matter where we are in our lives, Jesus always meets us there, to lead us forth into deeper faith, hope, and love. That he chose to do this with a Samaritan, and a woman at that, surprised the apostles. They could not understand that all souls are precious in the eyes of God.

- Spend some time with the passage, "Everyone who drinks this water will be thirsty again; but whoever drinks the water I shall give will never thirst; the water I shall give will become in him a spring of water welling up to eternal life" (John 4:13-14). What is the "water" that Jesus wants to share with the woman? How do you experience this "water" in your own life?

- "We no longer believe because of your word; for we have heard for ourselves, and we know that this is truly the savior of the world" (John 4:42). How do you experience the truth of this verse in your life?

- Pray for the grace to be open to ongoing conversion.

CYCLE B

Psalm 19:8-11
John 2:13-25: *Cleansing the Temple*

Jesus was outraged at the "business" of the Temple, which tended to exploit the poor and encourage superstition. The popular image of "Jesus meek and mild" is shattered in these verses as he single-handedly drives people and cattle out of the Temple precincts. When it comes to injustice, God is not meek and accepting.

- Jesus used his anger to act effectively. How do you express your anger?

- What injustice are you most aware of at this time in your life? How will you choose to stand against it?

- Pray for the grace to hunger and thirst for justice.

CYCLE C

Psalm 103:1-11
Luke 13:1-9: *Diligence and patience*

Two different points are made in this passage. The first is that people don't always get what they deserve—that bad things sometimes happen to good people, and vice versa. The second is that God is patient with us. Therefore, we should not judge people by the external appearances of their lives.

30

- Do you believe that some people are lucky, while others are unlucky? Why, or why not?

- Consider some examples of God's patience as recounted in Scripture. How do you experience God's patience in your own life?

- Pray for the grace to be patient with others.

Monday of the Third Week of Lent

Psalm 42:2-3;43:3-4
Luke 4:24-30: *A confrontation in Nazareth*

Since Jesus grew up in Nazareth, it is understandable that the people of his town thought they knew him better than most. They could not accept his special ministry, however, so Jesus confronted them for their lack of faith.

- Have you ever felt boxed-in or limited by close friends and family members who are interested only in that part of you with which they are comfortable? What is your response to this?

- Is there some friend or family member whom you need to get to know better? Resolve to communicate with that person about something new this week.

Tuesday of the Third Week of Lent

Psalm 25:4-9
Matthew 18:21-35: *The depths of forgiveness*

Today's reading continues the development of a theme that runs throughout the entire season of Lent—that of forgiveness and reconciliation. Jesus' admonition to forgive seventy-seven or seventy-times-seven times is not to be taken literally, of course: he is simply using exaggeration to make an important point.

- Is there anyone in your life you need to forgive? Ask for the grace to think of a creative way to let that person know that you forgive him or her.

- Is there anyone in your life whom you feel owes you forgiveness? Is reconciliation with this person possible?

Wednesday of the Third Week of Lent

Psalm 147:12-20
Matthew 5:17-19: *God's commandments are eternal*

Jesus taught that God's commandments were given to us not that we might analyze or evaluate their worth in terms of our own desires, but rather to help form those desires. Hence, God's commandments are to be obeyed.

- With which of God's commandments do you struggle most often? How will this struggle probably take place today?

- Pray for the grace to become more obedient to God's commandments.

Thursday of the Third Week of Lent

Psalm 95:1-2,6-9
Luke 11:14-23: *The reign of God is upon you*

The gospels reveal that it was impossible for people to encounter Jesus and remain indifferent toward him. This passage shows that some people interpreted his influence and power as arising from demonic sources. Jesus exposed the irrationality of their accusation and invited them to join him in gathering the kingdom harvest.

- What do you believe it means to be "with" Jesus? Whom do you believe is with him?

- What kind of conscience guards the doors of your soul? List some of the values that are most important to you.

Friday of the Third Week of Lent

Psalm 81:6-17
Mark 12:28-34: *The greatest commandment*

True religion is much simpler than we usually make it. In this passage, Jesus teaches us that God is not a philosophical proposition to be figured out, but a Being to be loved. Likewise, other human beings are to be loved even as we love ourselves.

- Make a list of the people and things you love most in this world, according to their importance to you. Where does God come in? How can you draw closer to God?

- Do you love yourself? How does your self-love affect your relationships?

Saturday of the Third Week of Lent

Psalm 51:3-4,18-21
Luke 18:9-14: *The Pharisee and the tax collector*

In this parable of contrasts, we get an idea of what our attitude toward God should be. Because everything we have and are and ever will be is made possible by grace, we should approach God in humble thanksgiving.

- Hear the Pharisee saying, "O God, I thank you that I am not like the rest of humanity" (Luke 18:11). Does this attitude resonate in you? Which people or groups of people do you believe you are superior to?

- Spend some time with the tax collector's prayer, "O God, be merciful to me a sinner" (Luke 18:13). As you breathe slowly, repeat this prayer again and again, allowing the words to draw you to God's mercy.

FOURTH WEEK OF LENT

Fourth Sunday of Lent

CYCLE A

Psalm 23
John 9:1-41: *A blind man sees*

Here again we see Jesus meeting a person where he is and leading him to conversion. In order to reveal God's glory, Jesus blesses the blind man with the gifts of sight and faith. The latter enables him to see Jesus as the Christ, or Anointed, of God.

- What prevents you from seeing goodness in yourself and others? Ask Jesus to rub your spiritual eyes with the grace of healing, so that you might see as he sees.

- The faith of the blind man enabled him to stand with courage in the face of adversity. Think of a situation in which you find it difficult to be true to your faith. Pray for the grace to remain faithful, and in your imagination, see yourself doing so.

CYCLE B

Psalm 137:1-6
John 3:14-21: *God so loved the world...*

Jesus teaches that he came not to judge us but to set up a standard by which we might judge ourselves. Those who live in the light of Christ will be drawn to God, while those who hate the truth will avoid God and condemn themselves accordingly.

- What does it mean, in the context of this reading, to "believe in Christ"? Are you a believer?

- How do you feel about God witnessing your entire life? What do you hope for from God?

- Pray for the grace to become a lover of the light.

CYCLE C

Psalm 34:2-7
Luke 15:1-3,11-32: *The prodigal son*

This parable appears only in the Gospel of Luke, who emphasizes the patience and mercy of God more than the other evangelists. It is a story that can be interpreted on many levels, but always it is the father who is the hero. Whether we are faithful or lost, the Father of Jesus loves us and wants us to be members of his family.

- How are you like the lost son? the faithful son? the father?

- Pray for the grace of a compassionate heart.

Monday of the Fourth Week of Lent

Psalm 30:2-6,11-13
John 4:43-54: *The official's son is healed*

The royal official in this reading was a Gentile, a non-Jew, but his faith in Jesus' ability to heal his sick boy transcended all racial and creedal boundaries. This is the kind of simple faith to which we are called.

- Picture in your imagination the scene between Jesus and the official. Hear the man continue pleading, despite Jesus' objections. See Jesus' face as he recognizes the great faith the official has in him.

- Rise from your prayer position and begin walking slowly around the room. With each step you take, believe that God will grant you the strength to persevere in love through any problems you might be having now. After a while, relax again, and give thanks to God for the gift of faith.

Tuesday of the Fourth Week of Lent

Psalm 46:1-9
John 5:1-3,5-16: *A healing in Jerusalem*

Jesus found people in great suffering and abandonment everywhere. In today's reading, he observes the faith and hope of a man who had been suffering for thirty-eight years. Jesus heals him but is criticized for doing so on the sabbath, a day when such works were forbidden.

- What "moving waters" are you waiting for so that you can get about the business of living fully? How is this affecting you now?

- Hear Jesus saying to you, "Rise, take up your mat, and walk" (John 5:8).

Wednesday of the Fourth Week of Lent

Psalm 145:8-9,13-14,17-18
John 5:17-30: *Jesus' credentials*

When the Jews criticized Jesus for healing on the sabbath, he replied that his Father, who goes on working always, is not bound by sabbath restrictions. He went on to invite the Jews to recognize that the power at work in him is critical to life and death.

- Read this passage again very slowly, spending time with whatever verses catches your attention. Do not try to reflect on every phrase.

- Spend some time with the words, "I do not seek my own will but the will of the one who sent me" (John 5:30). Repeat them again and again as you allow your will to merge with God's.

Thursday of the Fourth Week of Lent

Psalm 106:19-23
John 5:31-47: *More on Jesus' credentials*

When Jesus claimed to be doing God's work, it was only natural that the Jews should ask him for proof that this was in fact the case. Crackpots and false messiahs abounded then as now. Jesus pointed to the testimony of Moses and John the Baptist, of Scripture, and of the works that he did as evidence that his claims were not unfounded.

- What kind of reasoning supports your own faith in Jesus? How can you deepen your understanding of who Jesus is?

- What does human approval mean to you? How important is it in your involvement in the Church?

- Pray for the grace to be more detached from the need for human approval.

Friday of the Fourth Week of Lent

Psalm 34:17-23
John 7:1-2,10,25-30: *On Christ's origins*

The Jews had many preconceptions as to where the Messiah would come from, what he would be like, and what he would do. Many of these preconceptions prevented them from recognizing Jesus as the one they had prayed for.

- Have you, like Jesus, ever been misjudged and limited by others who drew hasty conclusions about you? Is this happening on a regular basis even now? How are you handling it?

- What do you do to prevent your first impressions about other people from limiting your relationship with them?

- Pray for the grace to let God be God in your life.

Saturday of the Fourth Week of Lent

Psalm 7:2-3,9-12
John 7:40-53: *The people's response to Jesus*

It was obvious to many people that Jesus was an extraordinary man. Still, they tried to cast him in every other role except the one which he himself proposed: that of God's Son.

- What do you think the temple guards experienced as they listened to Jesus? Have you ever experienced this? Get in touch with those memories and feelings.

- Resolve to do something special in the next week to help you draw closer to God.

FIFTH WEEK OF LENT

Fifth Sunday of Lent

CYCLE A

Psalm 130
John 11:1-45: *Jesus raises Lazarus from the dead*

To demonstrate fully his power over life and death, Jesus permitted the dead body of Lazarus to lay in the tomb for four days before calling him back to life. There could be no explaining away this miracle by claiming that Lazarus had only been unconscious or that Jesus was a magician. Clearly, the power of God was at work in him, for only God rules the portals of life and death.

- After reading through this passage, try to picture the events in your mind from a disciple's point of view. What are your feelings as you observe the unfolding of this story?

- Spend some time with the passage, "I am the resurrection and the life; whoever believes in me, even if he dies, will live, and everyone who lives and believes in me will never die. Do you believe this?" (John 11:25-26). What is your response to Jesus' question?

- Pray for loved ones who have died.

CYCLE B

Psalm 51:3-4,12-15
John 12:20-33: *Predictions of passion and resurrection*

In some mysterious way, Jesus knew when his earthly existence was coming to a close. While he was troubled by the agony he would have to endure, he was also eager to fulfill the work of reconciliation he had come to establish.

- What do you understand your work or mission to be at this time in your life?

- Spend some time with the verse, "The Father will honor whoever serves me" (John 12:26). How do you experience the Father honoring you for your work or mission?

- Pray for the grace to live your life with a sense of purpose.

CYCLE C

Psalm 126
John 8:1-11: *The woman caught in adultery*

Time and again, the Jewish authorities sought to entrap Jesus. In today's reading, they try to force him to choose between justice and mercy. Jesus avoided the trap by confronting their self-righteousness and restoring the woman to dignity.

- Have you ever been judged or condemned by others without cause? Recall what that felt like, and see if you can identify with the woman in today's gospel.

- Have you ever judged or condemned someone without cause? If so, how did you come to discover your error?

- Pray for the grace to see the goodness in others.

Monday of the Fifth Week of Lent

Psalm 23
John 8:1-11: *Jesus and the adulterous woman*

Today's reading reveals the depths of human malice that sickened Jesus. Having caught a woman (where was the man?) in the act of adultery, the authorities brought her to Jesus, attempting to pit his mercy against his justice and catch him in a trap. A pious tradition has it that when Jesus traced in the dirt, he spelled out the sins of the self-righteous accusers, causing them to depart shamefaced.

- In your imagination, put yourself in the place of a bystander observing this scene between the authorities, Jesus, and the woman. Note the self-righteousness on the face of the authorities; watch Jesus writing on the ground and glancing up at each official in turn; see the gratitude in the woman's eyes; hear Jesus speaking words of forgiveness to her.

- Write down your impressions from the imagination exercise. Note especially your impressions of Jesus.

Tuesday of the Fifth Week of Lent

Psalm 102:2-3,16-21
John 8:21-30: *Jesus is one with the Father*

Unlike Matthew, Mark, and Luke, John often has Jesus involved in long, profound dialogues with unbelievers and authorities, a device John used to articulate his community's understanding of who Jesus is in the face of persecution from Jews and Romans alike. In today's reading, Jesus speaks of the revelation that is to come when he is lifted up, or crucified.

- Spend some time with the passage, "The one who sent me is with me. He has not left me alone" (John 8:29). Become aware of God's nearness and love for you.

- Resolve to let a special person in your life know that you care about him or her.

Wednesday of the Fifth Week of Lent

Daniel 3:52-56
John 8:31-42: *The meaning of freedom*

It is a paradox that untamed passions bring enslavement, whereas self-discipline brings freedom. Jesus promises that the discipline of living according to his teaching will bring freedom, for he is the Son who reveals to us the human way to God.

- What does freedom mean to you? What kinds of situations restrict your experience of freedom? What are some of the limits of your exercise of freedom?

- Make a resolution to discipline a passion that has caused you loss of freedom. Pray for the grace to gain control of this passion.

Thursday of the Fifth Week of Lent

Psalm 105:4-9
John 8:51-59: *The eternal origin of the Christ*

The meeting of the human and divine in the person of Jesus shall forever be a mystery, an inexhaustible truth. Certainly, the human Jesus was born of Mary in space and time. John, however, reminds us today that the great I AM (Yahweh), whose knowledge is of eternity, also lives in Jesus. The Jews considered such a belief blasphemous and attempted to stone Jesus.

- What does today's reading have to say to those who consider Jesus to have been only a great man, or one of several incarnations of God, along with Buddha and Mohammed, for example?

- Spend some time with the passage, "If I glorify myself, my glory is worth nothing; but it is my Father who glorifies me" (John 8:54). Write your impressions.

Friday of the Fifth Week of Lent

Psalm 18:2-7
John 10:31-42: *Jesus confronts his critics*

Before the Jews rush to hasty conclusions, Jesus again reminds them that his works confirm his words, and he invites them to reconsider their unfounded judgments against him. When they reply by trying to arrest him, he escapes, for he is not yet ready to make his decisive confrontation.

- To whom do your works testify? To whom do you give the glory?

- Spend some time with the passage, "The Father is in me and I am in the Father" (John 10:38) and its parallel in the First Letter of John, "The one who is in you is greater than the one who is in the world" (4:4). Pray for the grace to be filled with the power of this presence.

Saturday of the Fifth Week of Lent

Jeremiah 31:10-13
John 11:45-57: *Jesus is condemned to die*

This passage comes after the raising of Lazarus, an event which caused many Jews to put their faith in Jesus. The Sanhedrin was a great religious council, a gathering of prominent spiritual leaders similar to our own bishops' conference today. Caiaphas, the designated leader, proposed that killing Jesus was preferable to the destruction of the status quo. John turns this statement into a cryptic prophecy of Jesus' redemptive death and resurrection.

- Russian novelist Leo Tolstoy wrote, "If, by doing God's will, I help to bring about the dissolution of the existing order of things, then the existing order of things needs to be changed." How does this statement differ from that of Caiaphas? Is there a middle ground between the two upon which a Christian might stand in good faith?

- Do you believe that any of the civil laws of your government conflict with the values of Christ? What stand do you take in such conflicts?

HOLY WEEK

Passion (Palm) Sunday

CYCLE A

Psalm 22:8-9,17-24
Matthew 26:14–27:66: *The passion and death of Jesus*

Since the Gospel of Matthew was written for a Jewish-Christian audience, the author takes every opportunity to draw connections between the life of Jesus and Hebrew Scripture. It was important for Matthew's audience to see that even Jesus' suffering and death were a fulfillment of Scripture, and not merely a human tragedy.

- The glorious risen Lord will forever be the same one who endured the suffering and death described in this narrative. Ask him to be with you in a special way as you read slowly through these verses. When you come to a word or phrase that speaks to you, pause awhile to converse with the Lord in your own words.

- Pray for the grace to join your own sufferings and struggles with those of Christ and to carry them as he did.

CYCLE B

Psalm 22:8-9,17-24
Mark 14:1–15:47: *The passion and death of Jesus*

This is the "hour" of the Son of Man. Now has the seed been planted in the earth, yet never was the sowing more cruelly done.

- Read this passage slowly and reverently, pausing to speak to Christ in your own words when you feel moved to do so.

- Jesus was tried, tortured, and executed by legitimate authorities from religious and political institutions. Do you think such unjust practices still go on?

- Pray for the grace to take a stand against evil.

CYCLE C

Psalm 22:8-9 17-24
Luke 22:14–23:56: *The passion according to Saint Luke*

In Luke's account of the passion and death of Jesus, the mercy of Christ is emphasized until the very end. As you read through this account, be attentive to the different insults and torments that Jesus' accusers inflict upon him. How does Jesus respond to them? Go and do the same.

Monday of Holy Week

Psalm 27:1-3,13-14
John 12:1-11: *Mary anoints Jesus*

We begin Holy Week with a reading that anticipates Jesus' death and burial. Earlier in John's Gospel, Mary had chosen to sit at Jesus' feet, while Martha, her sister, criticized her for not helping with the housework. In today's passage, Judas criticizes Mary for her extravagant expression of love for Jesus, but Jesus rebukes him and attests that her gesture is prophetic of his burial.

- Do you believe that money and time spent on Christian art and worship space are scandalous in a world where so many are poor? Why or why not?

- Make a resolution to demonstrate your love for another person in an extravagant way, for the glory of God.

Tuesday of Holy Week

Psalm 71:1-6,15-17
John 13:21-33,36-38: *Judas betrays Jesus*

It is very likely that Judas was a man with many admirable qualities, else Jesus would not have chosen him to be an apostle. Judas did not like the way things were turning out, however, and probably hoped that the confrontation he was forcing between Jesus and the authorities would put some "sense" into Jesus. Judas' plan backfired, as we know, but Jesus saw his betrayal as the beginning of his hour of glory.

- What are some of the ways in which you betray Jesus? Make a list, and ask God's forgiveness.

- Spend some time with the passage, "Where I am going, you cannot follow me now, though you will follow later" (John 13:36).

Wednesday of Holy Week

Psalm 69:8-10,21-22,31-34
Matthew 26:14-25: *The Passover meal begins*

The Passover is a Jewish feast recalling the liberation and exodus of the Jews from the land of Egypt. Jesus deeply loved this tradition and chose to share it with his most intimate friends, the apostles. This particular Passover meal will take on a new meaning in the light of Jesus' passion, death, and resurrection.

- How important to you is the sharing of a meal with friends and/or family? How does the sharing of a meal help to build relationships?

- Look into the possibility of sharing a Passover meal with a church group or some other community.

TRIDUUM

Holy Thursday

MASS OF THE LORD'S SUPPER

Psalm 116:12-18
John 13:1-15: *Jesus washes the apostles' feet*

This is Jesus' final evening with his apostles. It is a time to exchange farewells and prepare for the treachery to come. While the other evangelists emphasize the sharing of bread and wine as the memorial of Christ's death and resurrection, John recalls the *novum mandatum*, the "new commandment," in which Jesus washes his disciples' feet, the last symbolic intimacy he shares with them.

- Bishop Fulton J. Sheen once wrote that although we have Jesus' example of washing the apostles' feet as a model of service, it is difficult to find people today fighting for the towel. Is this true of you? What are some of the "lowly" jobs at home and at work you avoid because you feel they are "beneath your dignity?"

- Pray for the grace to be washed clean of false pride.

Good Friday

Psalm 31:2,6,12-17,25
John 18:1–19:42: *Jesus arrested, condemned, crucified*

Roman crucifixion was not the kind of death a community would choose for its hero. It was reserved for the most heinous criminals in society and was intended to discourage other would-be lawbreakers from testing the Pax Romana. Since the Jews were not permitted to carry out the death sentence, they needed to convince the Roman procurator, Pontius Pilate, that Jesus deserved to die. Though Pilate seems to have been reluctant to comply, he finally gave in, and Jesus was "lifted up."

- After reading through John's Passion narrative, spend some time reflecting on the cost of loving as Jesus loved.

- Dietrich Bonhoeffer, a Protestant minister executed by the Nazis for his complicity in the resistance movement, once wrote that when Jesus Christ calls a person, he bids him or her to come and die. How do you feel about this?

- Pray for the grace to be willing to lay down your life today for the sake of love.

Easter Vigil

CYCLE A

Psalm 104:1-6,10-15,24
Matthew 28:1-10: *Easter Sunday morning*

The empty tomb was a fact that not even the Jewish authorities disputed. Yet this alone did not convince the women or the disciples that the Lord had risen. He revealed himself to them in a way that proved he was truly alive, yet alive in a manner much more wonderful than before.

- After reading through this passage, close your eyes and journey with the women to the tomb. Feel their anguish as they go to anoint the body, note their bewilderment when they see the angel, and share their joy when they encounter the risen Christ.

- Pray for the grace to be free from the fear of death.

CYCLE B

Psalm 42:3-5;43:3-4
Mark 16:1-8: *The women at the tomb*

Mark's is the earliest written account available to us today of the events of Easter Sunday. The women who loved Jesus most were the first to learn that he had risen. They were also the first evangelists, since they were given the commission to share this good news.

- Try to imagine what it would be like not to believe in life after death. How would this affect your sense of life's meaning or your hope for the future?

- For you, what is the significance of the Resurrection?

- Pray for the grace to long for your heavenly home.

CYCLE C

Psalm 51:12-19
Luke 24:1-12: *Christ is risen*

It has often been said that the Good News is too good to be true. This seemed to be the opinion of the apostles upon hearing the news brought by the women. Yet who would have expected such a wonder as the Resurrection? Truly, the goodness of God far exceeds our feeble expectations.

- The late Frank Sheed wrote that, too often, we fail to appreciate the truths of our faith because we have heard them so many times that we now listen to them in a "pious coma." Put yourself in the place of the apostles as they first heard the news of the Resurrection. Try to get in touch with Peter's amazement at the empty tomb. Could it really be true?

- Pray for the grace to be open to the wonders of God.

Easter Sunday

Psalm 118:1-2,16-17,22-23
John 20:1-9: *Journey to the empty tomb*

Although John's Gospel features much theological reflection, it also includes many details from the life of Jesus. This account of the empty tomb is that of an eyewitness who describes for us what he saw when he went into the tomb. Note John's deference to the leadership of Peter in allowing him to enter the tomb before him.

- After entering the empty tomb, John "saw and believed." What would help you to believe more deeply in the Resurrection?

- The tomb stood empty. Spend some time listening to Jesus tell you where he can now be found.

- Pray for the grace to see God in all things.